# THE BATTLE OF VERDUN

The Horror of Trench Warfare

Written by Romain Parmentier
Translated by Carly Probert

History 50MINUTES.com

# THE BATTLE OF VERDUN

## KEY INFORMATION

- **When:** 21 February-19 December 1916
- **Where:** Verdun, France
- **Context:** The First World War (1914-1918)
- **Belligerents:** France against the German Empire
- **Commanders and leaders:**
    - Philippe Pétain, French general (1856-1951)
    - Erich von Falkenhayn, German general (1861-1922)
- **Outcome:** French victory
- **Victims:**
    - French camp: approximately 146 000 dead or missing and 216 000 injured
    - German camp: approximately 140 000 dead or missing and 196 000 injured

## INTRODUCTION

A historic engagement of the First World War, the Battle of Verdun was nevertheless one of the most atrocious and inhumane battles in history.

The attack began on 21 February 1916 at 7:15am, ordered by German Chief of the General Staff Erich von Falkenhayn, who wanted to end the war of position and "bleed the French army dry". Since November 1914, the war of movement, which involved advancing as far as possible into enemy territory in order to gain ground, was no longer current. The armies were trapped in trenches dug into the ground and neither of them managed to gain an advantage. The conflict became a war of position where each defended the sector that had been assigned to them.

By launching an attack on Verdun, the Germans hoped to change this situation and achieve a victory over the French army. Thus, the French and the Germans were locked in a fierce battle for nearly ten months, which could have determined the outcome of the war. However, contrary to the expectations of the Germans, the French soldiers, now nicknamed the "Poilus" (literally meaning "the hairy ones"), resisted with the support of their general, Philippe Pétain. In the lunar hell of Verdun, they eventually defeated the Germans, but suffered significant losses, and in the end the battle turned out to be a useless massacre.

# POLITICAL AND SOCIAL CONTEXT

## THE PREMISES OF THE FIRST WORLD WAR

Far from being an isolated event, the Battle of Verdun was part of a much broader military context: the First World War. This conflict, later called the "Great War", was primarily fought between the central powers of Germany and Austria-Hungary, the Triple Alliance, and the coalition of France, Great Britain and the Russian Empire, united as the Triple Entente, between 1914 and 1918. Subsequently, many countries declared themselves at war due to interplays of alliances and support, transforming the conflict into a global affair.



The Triple Alliance was created in 1882 and aimed to unite Germany, Austria-Hungary and Italy. There are several reasons for this rally:

- Germany wanted to isolate France, which had become more and more hostile since the Franco-Prussian war (1870-1871);
- Austria-Hungary saw it as an opportunity to obtain allies to counter Russian expansionism in the Balkans;
- Italy wanted to be stronger against French colonialism.

In response to this, the Triple Entente was established

in 1907. It brought together Great Britain, Russia and France and aimed to counter the expansionist policy of Germany. Early in the conflict, Italy decided to leave the Triple Alliance, claiming that it had not been consulted before the declaration of war by Austria-Hungary, and declared itself neutral. However, in May 1915, Italy entered the war on the Allied side, thus signaling the end of the Triple Alliance.

In 1914, Europe experienced an unprecedented crisis resulting from several tensions:

- economic rivalries among states;
- expansionist and imperialist aims from certain countries;
- nationalist outbreaks in the Balkans (peninsula of Southern Europe, bounded by the Danube, Sava and Kupa);
- alliances between state powers.

All of these factors seemed only able to provoke widespread conflict. It only took one trigger to set things off.

This trigger occurred on 28 June 1914, with the assassination of Archduke Franz Ferdinand of Habsburg (1863-1914), heir to the Austrian throne, in Sarajevo. This attack demonstrated the extreme tension prevailing at that time in South East Europe. As a continually coveted territory, the Balkans became the scene of rivalries between the Austro-Hungarian, Ottoman and Russian Empires. This is also where Slavic nationalism appeared, which was particularly present in Serbia. At the time, Bosnia-Herzegovina – of which Sarajevo is the capital – was under Austro-Hungarian rule, causing strong protests to arise in Serbia, calling for the unification of the Slav populations within one state, which would later become Yugoslavia. It was discovered soon after that the attack was perpetrated by a young Serbian nationalist from Bosnia, Gavrilo Princip (1894-1918), who wanted to protest against the Austro-Hungarian presence in the Balkans. Although an isolated act, this assassination is seen as the trigger for the First World War, as it was responsible for the activation of the alliance mechanisms.

*Assassination of Archduke Franz Ferdinand of Austria and his wife Sophie von Hohenberg* by a Serb, on 28 June 1914. Illustration from French newspaper *Le Petit Journal*.

The agreements made between states (the Triple Alliance and the Triple Entente) promptly made a regional dispute into a generalized war. Once the Serbian responsibility in the attack of 28 June was recognized, the Austro-Hungarian Empire issued an ultimatum to Serbia on 23 July. However,

Serbia refused the cooperation of the Austrian police in the investigation aiming to find those responsible for the attack. Indeed, accepting such a condition would have undermined Serbian sovereignty. The consequences of this refusal were quick to follow: on 28 July, Austria-Hungary, strengthened by German support, declared war on Serbia. Russia, considering itself to be a protector of the Slavs and an ally of Serbia, declared the general mobilization of its army. Germany then saw this as an opportunity to impose its interests on Europe and consequently declared war on Russia on 1 August, counting on its alliance with Austria.

The German Empire then posed an ultimatum to France to ensure its neutrality, but France refused to comply and began to mobilize. From then on, Germany developed a strategy based on the Schlieffen Plan (named after its creator Alfred, Count von Schlieffen, a German marshal, 1833-1913). This plan was developed between 1898 and 1905 (i.e. a few years after the Franco-Russian alliance), and detailed a tactic that aimed to attack and beat France in only a few weeks and then fight Russia, its ally. The commander in chief of the German army decided to apply the principles of this plan and prepared to launch an attack on France before Russia began fighting in the east. Once France was defeated, German troops would then be transferred to fight Russia. To achieve this objective, Germany issued an ultimatum to Belgium in order to allow the army to march through the country, but Belgium refused. Then, on 3 August, Germany declared war on France and attacked Belgium the following day. A guarantor of Belgian neutrality, Britain entered into the conflict by declaring war on Germany.

While the conflict was originally essentially European, the search for allies transformed it into a world war over time.

## FROM A WAR OF MOVEMENT TO A WAR OF TRENCHES

The First World War began to unfold just like any other conflict, namely as a war of movement. The enemy troops tried to move as quickly and as far as possible into enemy lands in order to seize the territory. This was what Germany aimed to do by implementing the Schlieffen Plan and it hoped to quickly defeat France and then turn against Russia. A victory over both enemies would ensure the economic and territorial expansion of its empire.

It was with this aim that the German Chief of the General Staff, Helmuth Johannes von Moltke (1848-1916) implemented the war plan in August 1914 by invading Belgium. He was certain that the Belgian army, which was badly organized, would not hold up against them. Contrary to these assumptions, the Belgian soldiers resisted and managed to delay the German attack by eight days. This time period allowed the French and the British soldiers to enter Belgium to counter the German army. Nevertheless, the horror of the fighting, the lack of training of the French army, their aging military strategy, and the inadequate use of artillery gradually forced the Allies to retreat. The German advance continued on Paris and therefore, on 2 September 1914, the enemy invaded the Department of the Marne, causing the French government to transfer to Bordeaux. Undeterred, General Joseph Joffre (1852-1931), commander of the French army, ordered the troops to resist in the Marne and launched a counter-attack.



The Battle of the Marne was a victory for the French who had forced the Germans to retreat. Gradually, the front line stabilized and, faced with heavy firepower and the extreme violence of the fighting, the armies buried themselves in the trenches. The war of movement was over, giving way to trench warfare.

German soldiers on the front of the First Battle of Marne.

## SOCIO-ECONOMIC CONSEQUENCES

From the beginning of the conflict, everyday life was affected in the belligerent countries. In fact, the war required significant material and human forces. In full harvest, the French were forced to join the army. The industrial sector was also deserted. Therefore, all economic activity slowed down.

The end of the war of movement did nothing but heighten this disruption. Although the war was only intended to last a few months, it got bogged down in the trenches which suggested the possibility of a much longer conflict. This caused inevitable consequences in terms of supply: communication channels were requisitioned for the benefit of transporting weapons and supplies to the front, which greatly disadvantaged trade. The war was now affecting the different sectors of society. It could now be referred to as a total war.

The situation was even more critical for Germany, which was at risk of economic strangulation. Its economy, largely based on the industrial sector, was indeed dependent on imports of raw materials. The agriculture sector was also heavily affected and the German Empire alone could not ensure subsistence. Furthermore, the Allies did not fail to exploit the situation by imposing a trade blockade and preventing any country, even those that were neutral, from procuring raw materials on its behalf. This had negative consequences for society: seeing their living standards decline, the Germans would eventually challenge the war. In 1917, the country narrowly avoided a communist revolution similar to the one that took place in Russia later that year. For Germany, exiting the war soon became an emergency.

In 1917, Russia was in total crisis. The soldiers sent to the front were lacking in weapons and the country's situation was catastrophic. Life was becoming more and more expensive, making it impossible for people to eat. Demonstrations and strikes broke out in Petrograd (St. Petersburg) in February, then spread around the country. The people were uprising and, in March, part of the army rallied the protesting workers, allowing them to obtain weapons. Powerless in the face of the events that were tearing his country apart, Tsar Nicolas II (1868-1918) abdicated in favor of his brother, who refused the throne. A provisional government was then set up. But the situation was far from resolved due to the opposition between the bourgeois and popular powers. Soon, Russian revolutionary Lenin (1870-1924) re-launched the fighting and triggered the October Revolution. The coup led to the creation of the Russian Soviet Federative Socialist Republic and the communist regime.

## VERDUN: A STRATEGIC LOCATION FOR GERMANY

Faced with the risk of an economic crisis, Germany realized that it must end the war as soon as possible. The empire therefore sought to negotiate peace on its own terms with several countries, but the various negotiations failed. Therefore, the only solution that remained to end the conflict was to see it through and win.

General Erich von Falkenhayn, who replaced Helmuth Johannes von Moltke after the failure at the Battle of the Marne, established a plan of attack for the Western Front from December 1915. It involved forcing France into a battle of attrition which would gradually destroy its reserves. The only thing left to do was to find the place where such a fight would occur: Verdun.

The city of Verdun was chosen as it was a strategic objective. Indeed, it was the cornerstone of the French front and also had a sentimental value for France, which could not bring itself to abandon it. It offered many opportunities for the Germans:

- The French front drew a salient around the city, allowing the German army to attack its flanks;
- The Meuse runs through the city, cutting the field in half, making the defense of the city more difficult. Stuck in the valley, it could be dominated by German artillery;
- Only a single communication line allowed for the sending of French supplies, while the Verdun area was well served by railways on the German side, facilitating supply;
- Forts located in the city were not sufficiently protected. General Joseph Joffre had exhausted much of his artillery in other fights.

Through this attack, the German commander was hoping to attract the French forces, defeat them and, in the words of Erich von Falkenhayn, "bleed them dry" (Association nationale du souvenir de la bataille de Verdun, 1976: 55).

Such an operation would result in the surrendering of the French and force them to sign a peace agreement according to German conditions. After that, the British in the West would not last long.

# COMMANDERS AND LEADERS

## PHILIPPE PÉTAIN, FRENCH GENERAL

Philippe Pétain was a French general who officiated during the Great War. When the conflict broke out, he was delivering lectures as a colonel in the War College and was approaching retirement. During his lessons, he offered his students completely innovative theories: he went against the military perceptions that prevailed until then by refusing the doctrine of "attaque à outrance" (French, meaning "attack to excess"), which stated that victory was gained through the massive engagement of armed troops. He based his ideas on a more logical concept: "Fire kills". (Le Naour, 2008: 346). He therefore prioritized the economizing of human lives and the increased use of artillery. The violence of the fighting in 1914 gave him reason and re-launched his military career. He was appointed brigadier general, then commander of a troop that participated in the Battle of the Marne.

The year of 1916 changed the status of Philippe Pétain. Given the brutality of the German attack, General Joseph Joffre put him in charge of the defense of Verdun, where the French army was in trouble. Philippe Pétain became its savior. He reinforced the only supply route of the city, which was given the name "the sacred path" and, concerned for morale, he organized the rotation of the armed divisions. He proved himself to be close to his soldiers and did not hesitate to encourage them, as confirmed by his command on 9 April 1916: "Courage! We will get them!" (*ibid.*: 348). His lack of offensive character nonetheless prompted his replacement in May 1916 by General Georges Robert Nivelle (1856-1824). Nivelle gradually pushed the Germans back and put an end to the battle in December 1916. However, history recognizes Philippe Pétain as the true victor of Verdun.

Subsequently, the command of Philippe Pétain extended to the central army groups and, in 1917, he became the head of the entire army. He had to face the consequences of Georges Robert Nivelle's failure at the Battle of Chemin des Dames and managed to avoid the collapse of the French army. Anxious to save as many lives as possible, he decided to wait for the arrival of the Americans before resuming the attack. After the armistice of 1918, Philippe Pétain was named Marshal of France.

## GOOD TO KNOW

The Chemin des Dames is a county road about thirty kilometers in length, between Aisne and Ailette. General Georges Robert Nivelle wanted to attack the Germans to gain ground on the enemy. But, the German General Erich Ludendorff (1865-1937) discovered the plans of the French thanks to the capture of a soldier. During the attack, the Germans were therefore very well prepared and fiercely fought the French who refused to give up. In the end, the Germans emerged victorious. The losses were numerous: there were approximately 40 000 deaths on the French side, while the German losses were less heavy, amounting to 21 000 soldiers lost, most of whom were captured.

However, Philippe Pétain's career did not stop there. With his popularity, he was recalled during the Second World War (1939-1945) and became War Minister and President of the Council. The outcome, however, was less pleasing. Concluding an armistice with the Germans in 1940, he became head of the Vichy regime (the capital of what remains of France) in the Free France area. This was followed by an increasingly advanced collaboration with the Nazi regime, including the deportation of Jews. In 1945, he was arrested by the new French authorities and sentenced to death by the High Court for treason. This sentence was commuted by Charles de Gaulle (French statesman, 1890-1970) to life detention on the island of Yeu, where he died in 1951.

## ERICH VON FALKENHAYN, GERMAN GENERAL

Erich von Falkenhayn was a German General who took part in the First World War. When the conflict broke out, he was Minister of War. Following the failure of General Helmuth Johannes von Moltke at the Battle of the Marne in September 1914, he became head of the High Command of the German army. Erich von Falkenhayn became infamous thanks to his several victories on the Eastern Front in 1915. However, he no longer believed in military victory, but rather a political peace that could be reached after having exhausted the enemy.

It was in this light that he planned the Battle of Verdun in December 1915. Convinced of the moral decay of the French soldiers, he decided to launch a war of attrition at Verdun.

He hoped to lure the French forces to that area in order to destroy them gradually through violent attacks, with no regard for human life. Despite the German advance in the first months of battle, the Verdun attack ended in failure. The French resistance reaped the rewards and led to the downfall of Erich von Falkenhayn's career. The latter was replaced in August 1916 by General Paul von Hindenburg (1847-1934). He nonetheless continued the war on the Eastern Front as a troop commander in Romania (1916) and Palestine (1917-1918). After the war, he wrote his memoirs and died in 1922 near Potsdam (Germany).

# ANALYSIS OF THE BATTLE

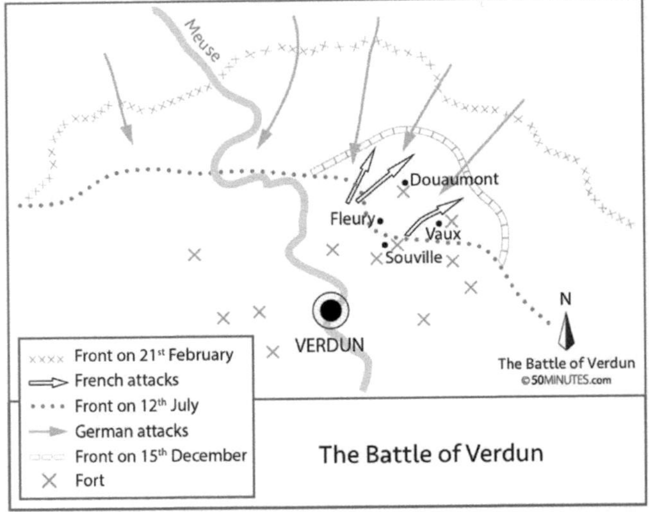



The Battle of Verdun

## PREPARATIONS

At first, the fortified town of Verdun seemed very well defended, even impregnable. It was surrounded by the mountains and hills of the Meuse valley. For protection, it had 19 forts and 19 important infantry works. The most important of these was the Fort Douaumont, which rose about 400 meters northeast of the city, near the right bank of the Meuse. However, this impression of power was only illusory. Indeed, in August 1915, convinced that the city would not be the object of attack, the French command decided to withdraw nearly 200 guns from the forts, leaving only 263. Moreover, the number of garrisons present on the site was also reduced to a dozen men.

On the German side, once Erich von Falkenhayn's plan had been approved, preparations for the attack of Verdun began. Leadership was assigned to the Prussian Crown Prince Frederick William (1882-1951), nicknamed the *Kronprinz* ("Crown Prince" in German). The attack was originally scheduled for 12 February 1916 and they decided to name it the *Gericht* (judgment). For the attack, 1 225 artillery pieces of all kinds were sent to Verdun. Meanwhile, trains were responsible for transporting two and a half million shells. Finally, 140 000 foot soldiers were requisitioned and converged in the sector. This preparation phase was delicate. It was indeed necessary to avoid attracting the attention of the French and keep the attack secret. The Germans therefore imposed their presence in the skies in order to avoid the French reconnaissance aircrafts. The only thing not considered by the German command was the weather. A storm delayed the attack by nine days. During this time, they needed to maintain secrecy, stay hidden and hope that no deserter would warn the opponent.

However, these measures did not remain unknown to the French. Indeed, the intelligence services noticed the bustle around the city and warned that an attack was possible. But nobody believed this. However, these warnings were corroborated by French soldiers at Verdun who could hear the preparations being made every day on the other side of the front. Taking precautions, General Joseph Joffre still sent two divisions, but the soldiers were ill-prepared and did not envisage the hell they were about to face. On 20 February, an Alsatian deserter warned the French that the attack was scheduled for the next day, but he was not taken seriously. It took a few days for General Joseph Joffre to become aware that the Battle of Verdun would be decisive.

## INTO THE GUNFIRE

At dawn on 21 February 1916, the Germans were guided by a simple idea: "The artillery will conquer, the infantry will occupy" (Association nationale du souvenir de la bataille de Verdun, 1976: 81). Indeed, this sentence was said by Philippe Pétain, but the fact remains that it was now this thought that guided the various belligerent armies, starting with the Germans. Using guns excessively, the Germans hoped to exhaust the French forces and clear the road of Verdun. At around 7:15am, a naval gun located thirty kilometers behind the German lines launched its first shell which landed in the courtyard of the bishopric of Verdun. This firing marked the beginning of continuous and at will bombing that lasted for more than nine hours. This was unprecedented in military history, especially since the attack zone only extended about ten kilometers. A material and savage war began, until everything seemed dead. The landscape surrounding Verdun was transformed in just one day. The surrounding woods were pulverized by shelling. The trenches were rutted and the barbed wire torn. The survivors, if there were any, were reduced to a state of madness by the incessant bombing, which is understandable given that more than one million shells fell on that first day.

Soldiers under canon fire in Verdun.

After the artillery, the German infantry entered onto the scene. Its mission was to take the first line of trenches and identify the second in a lunar landscape riddled with craters. Despite their inflexible will to resist, the French survivors could only delay the German advance, and were unable to push them back. To add to the horror of the situation, the Germans decided to use a new weapon on the French: the flamethrower, which reduced the soldiers to human torches. Rifles, bayonets, machine guns, grenades, mines, highly toxic gas – anything was allowed in Verdun. Helpless, the French were forced to abandon the first line of trenches to retreat to fortified positions. The German advance was certainly less significant than expected, but the mission for this first day was completed.

The attack continued the following day with the same

level of violence. On 24 February, only the forts and a few handfuls of men stood in the way of the Germans, but the Fort Douaumont was now exposed. It was attacked on 25 February. Preceded by artillery fire, the German soldiers swooped down on the fort and discovered a garrison of 60 older men there who surrendered without a fight. This victory resounded throughout Germany. Verdun was no further than seven kilometers. However, the French army had not had its final words.

## THE SAVIOR OF VERDUN

Faced with the disastrous situation of the French army, General Joseph Joffre sent the second army, whose commander was General Philippe Pétain, to Verdun's rescue. Pétain thus took over the left bank of the Meuse, but he was also responsible for directing the operations on the right bank, which needed to be defended at all costs. He decided to gather artillery and give the Germans a taste of their own medicine.

Arriving at the front on 26 February, Philippe Pétain also reorganized the logistics in only one day. With the railway line being too dilapidated for use, there was only one way to access Verdun. This was a small country road, barely six meters wide, linking Bar-le-Duc to Verdun. It was the only one that could supply the army and was later christened the "sacred path" by Maurice Barres (French writer and politician, 1862-1923). Philippe Pétain requisitioned 3 000 trucks from all over France and they circulated 24 hours a day, every day, bumper to bumper, to supply the army.

Approximately 6 000 journeys were made per day, which was one every 14 seconds.

To keep up morale, Philippe Pétain also organized rotations of troops so that in a few months, two-thirds of the French army fought at Verdun. This helped to confer the fight of an entire nation and participated in the collective memory of the horrors of the battlefield. The troops had time to rest, but the constant fear of returning to the horror was always present.

Troops replaced after the first encounter, on 26th February 1916.

Until then, Erich von Falkenhayn's plan had worked. The French army had focused on Verdun, but the German advance gradually slowed down and the losses were increasing in their ranks. In March, the French artillerymen continued to bomb the German lines on the left bank of the Meuse. The German command decided to launch an attack in the region and seize the hill called the "dead man's hill" and the coast 304 that led to Fort Vaux. The various attempts ended in failure. Thus, in late March, the German losses amounted to 80 607 victims – 7 000 fewer than the French. It was not until the beginning of May that the coast 304 – which was then only 297 meters long, instead of the initial 304 meters – fell to the Germans, following a bombardment of German artillery that was even more powerful than that which took place on 21 February. Soon after, "dead man's hill" was also taken by the Germans. However, the price of victory was shockingly high.

When summer returned, the living conditions of the soldiers became intolerable. Everywhere, bodies covered the floor, which was nothing more than a sea of mud. The heat made the air increasingly unbreathable due to the decomposition of the bodies shredded by the shells. Dysentery now affected the soldiers from both camps.

## THE OUTCOME OF THE BATTLE: A USELESS MASSACRE

In May, Joseph Joffre decided to replace Philippe Pétain with General Georges Robert Nivelle in order to opt for a more aggressive approach in Verdun and preserve reserves. Unlike his predecessor, Georges Robert Nivelle cared little about the loss of lives and launched a series of attacks, each one more lethal than the last. At this point, the battle was no longer controlled and each side continually harassed the other in a war of attrition.

In early June, the German advance continued nonetheless with the capture of Fort Vaux, guarded by 500 men, at the cost of fierce fighting against the French resistance. The next German objective was the Fort Souville. They reached it on 11 July and this was the culmination of the German advance. Faced with strong resistance from the French, the Germans did not go further and were even pushed out of Fort Souville the next day.

Meanwhile, a new front was created on 1 July in the region of Somme. This battle allowed for the changing of the strategic landscape of the front. Obliged to send troops in this sector, Erich von Falkenhayn was forced to place the Verdun army in a defensive position, and to reduce its size. This led to the fall of the general who was replaced by General Paul von Hindenburg on 29 August.

## GOOD TO KNOW

The Battle of the Somme took place from 1 July to 19 November 1916. It was launched by the French and British soldiers, on the orders of General Joseph Joffre, in order to relieve the Verdun front and seize strategic communication points. Their tactic was also to tire the German forces that were not ready to fight in this sector. In just five months, there were an estimated 1.2 million victims in total (dead, wounded or missing).

Paul von Hindenburg reorganized the German army in a strict defensive position on 2 September. This decision marked the failure of the Germans. From 24 October, the lost territory and the forts were recaptured one after the other by the French. On 15 December, a new French attack pushed the front line back three kilometers beyond the Fort Douaumont and on 19 December, the situation had returned to normal. The agony of Verdun ended with a French victory.

In the end, the gains of both sides were zero. Nobody took the lead and the massacre caused by the fighting was for nothing. The losses were heavy:

- In the French camp, 146 000 were killed and 216 000 wounded;
- On the German side, there were 140 000 dead and 196 000 wounded.

The Battle of Verdun therefore became the second bloo-diest battle of the First World War, after the Battle of the Somme. The strategy of Erich von Falkenhayn had "[bled] dry" (*ibid.*: 346) the French army just as much as the German army. His mistake was believing that the French would do as the German army expected, namely losing ground due to faltering morale. But in Verdun, a whole nation fought to defend France.

# REPERCUSSIONS OF THE BATTLE

## A BATTLE WITH SEVERE CONSEQUENCES

Today, historians are unanimous in describing the Battle of Verdun as a bloody aberration that led to the unnecessary slaughter of thousands of soldiers. Indeed, in addition to the losses incurred, the results were disastrous. At the end of the battle:

- No strategic shift had been made since the two camps had returned to their initial position;
- The German and French soldiers were exhausted and scarred by heavy wounds, to the point where people spoke of "broken faces" to describe the victims;
- The war was not about to end, contrary to German wishes.

Nevertheless, the Battle of Verdun had several consequences, including the outbreak of the Battle of the Somme in July 1916. This inflicted heavy losses to both the French and German armies, ultimately making any kind of victory on the Western Front impossible. The Battle of the Somme was initiated in parallel with the Battle of Verdun, namely in order to try to slow the German attack and thus attract the enemy onto another sector. This is now considered to be the deadliest battle of the First World War, since it is estimated today that there was a total of 1.2 million victims.

# THE UNITED STATES ENTERED THE WAR

These failures were significant for Germany, which risked economic strangulation because of its encirclement by the Entente powers. Therefore, in 1917, the German emperor, Wilhelm II (1859-1941), had no choice but to authorize unrestricted submarine warfare. In torpedoing any ship travelling to England, the German command hoped to discourage the British and bring them out of the war. Once the British set off the conflict, Germany could more easily bring an end to the French. However, far from discouraging the British, the submarine warfare eventually got the Americans involved in the conflict.

In 1914, the United States chose to remain neutral, but this position slowly evolved until 1917. Already in 1915, a German submarine had sunk a British civilian liner, the *Lusitania*, which was carrying 128 U.S. citizens, which upset public opinion in the United States. The policy of 1917 in Germany made things worse and the situation deteriorated even more as a result of a German attempt to involve Mexico in a war against the United States. The United States declared war on Germany on 2 April 1917, thereby changing the balance of forces on the Western Front, despite the end of the war in the east (with the Treaty of Brest-Litovsk ratified in March 1918 by the central powers).

One thing leading to another, the Battle of Verdun consequently amended German policy, leading to the involvement of the U.S. in the war. The war then took a different turn and precipitated the fall of the German Empire.

# A DEVASTATED SECTOR

In Verdun, the consequences of the battle were irreparable. Of course, the trees and grass grew back, but the landscape was forever marked by shell craters, some of which have not yet exploded. Several villages were even eradicated from the map after the battle. They are now reduced to ghost towns, completely uninhabited, often with only one chapel built after the battle.

Finally, the horror of Verdun which saw the deaths of so many French and German soldiers, became the symbol of the tragedies of the First World War. After the conflict, the construction of a memorial and an ossuary was also undertaken to remind everyone of the horror of the fighting. However, the slaughter of Verdun would not be enough to prevent the world from sinking into a new world conflict in 1939.

A few years later, like a repetition of history, the Battle of Stalingrad (17 July 1942-2 February 1943) ended the same way as Verdun: a German army attack failed in the face of Russian resistance, at the expense of a city that was completely destroyed and thousands of victims on both sides.

# SUMMARY

**1915**

*Dec.*: Erich von Falkenhayn planned the attack on Verdun

**1916**

*21st Feb.*: Attack on Verdun

*26th Feb.*: Arrival of Philippe Pétain on the front

*May*: Philippe Pétain is replaced by Georges Robert Nivelle

*1st July*: Start of the Battle of the Somme

*29th Aug.*: Erich von Falkenhayn is replaced by Paul von Hindenburg

*18th Nov.*: End of the Battle of the Somme

*19th Dec.*: End of the Battle of Verdun



- The Battle of Verdun in 1916 was a major battle of the First World War. This war began in 1914, following the assassination of the Archduke Franz Ferdinand in Sarajevo. The game of alliances between the European States ended up creating widespread conflict.

- Germany declared war on France and Russia. In order to avoid being faced with two fronts, it decided to first attack the French and beat them quickly.

- However, after a major breakthrough, the German army was stopped. The soldiers buried themselves in the trenches.

- In order to break this lack of movement, German General Erich von Falkenhayn decided to launch an attack on Verdun, the cornerstone of the French front.
- After several weeks of preparations, the attack was given on 21 February 1916. The first phase of the attack was the relentless bombarding of the field with artillery. For hours, guns fired around Verdun. Then the German infantry took over and pushed the French army back.
- Faced with this catastrophic situation, the French General gave the command to Philippe Pétain's army. The latter, the true savior of Verdun, organized the supply of ammunition and implemented a rotation of troops.
- The German advance continued until 11 July. However, the launch of the Battle of the Somme on 1 July and the fall of Erich von Falkenhayn in August marked the decline of the German attack at Verdun.
- Finally, the fronts returned to their starting positions. The battle is seen as an unnecessary massacre that caused considerable losses:
  - On the French side, there were 146 000 dead and 216 000 wounded;
  - On the German side, there were 140 000 dead and 196 000 wounded.

# FIND OUT MORE

## BIBLIOGRAPHY


- Chautard, S. and Féki, M. (2012) Verdun (21 février-18 décembre 1916). In Chautard, S. (ed.) *Les Grandes Batailles de l'histoire*. Nanterre: Studyrama.
- Genevoix. M et al. (1976) *Verdun 1916. Actes du colloque international sur la bataille de Verdun (6-7-8 juin 1975)*. Nancy: Association Nationale du Souvenir de la Bataille de Verdun.
- Hardier, T. and Jagielski, J.-F. (2001) *Combattre et mourir pendant la Grande Guerre. 1914-1925*. Paris: Imago.
- Krumeich, G. and Audoin-Rouzeau, S. (2004) Les Batailles de la Grande Guerre. In Becker, J.-J. and Audoin-Rouzeau, S. (eds.) *Encyclopédie de la Grande Guerre*. Paris: Bayard.
- Le Naour, J.-Y. (2008) Erich von Falkenhayn. *Dictionnaire de la Grande Guerre*. Paris: Larousse.
- Le Naour, J.-Y. (2008) Philippe Pétain. *Dictionnaire de la Grande Guerre*. Paris: Larousse.
- Le Naour, J.-Y. (2008) Verdun. *Dictionnaire de la Grande Guerre*. Paris: Larousse.
- Miquel, P. (1995) *Mourir à Verdun*. Paris: Tallandier.
- Prior, R. and Wilson, T. (2000) *The First World War*. London: Cassell.
- Site de la Communauté de Communes de Verdun et de la Ville de Verdun (No date). *La Bataille de Verdun*. [Online]. [Accessed 5 December 2016]. Available from: <http://www.verdun.fr/Terre-d-Histoire/Verdun-et-la-Grande-Guerre/La-Bataille-de-Verdun>

## ADDITIONAL SOURCES


- Axelrod, A. (2016) *The Battle of Verdun*. Guildford: Connecticut: Lyons Press.
- Horne, A. (1994) *The Price of Glory: Verdun 1916*. London: Penguin.
- Jankowski, P. (2014) *Verdun: The Longest Battle of the Great War*. Oxford: Oxford University Press.
- Mosier, M. (2013) *Verdun: The Lost History of the Most Important Battle of World War I, 1914-1918*. New York: NAL Caliber.


## ICONOGRAPHIC SOURCES


- *Assassination of Archduke Franz Ferdinand of Austria and his wife Sophie von Hohenberg by a Serb*, on 28 June 1914. Illustration from French newspaper *Le Petit Journal*. Royalty-free reproduction picture.
- German soldiers on the front of the First Battle of Marne.
- Soldiers under canon fire in Verdun. Royalty-free reproduction picture.
- Troops replaced after the first encounter, on 26 February 1916. Royalty-free reproduction picture.


## FILMS AND DOCUMENTARIES


- *Verdun, visions d'histoire*. (1928) [Documentary]. Léon Poirier. Dir. France: Compagnie Universelle Cinématographique.
- *Paths of Glory*. (1957) [Film]. Stanley Kubrick. Dir. USA:

Bryna Productions.
- *Die Hölle von Verdun.* (2006) [Documentary]. Olivier Halmburger and Stefan Brauburger. Dir. Germany: ZDF, Regie.
- *Le Siècle de Verdun.* (2006) [Documentary]. Patrick Barberis. Dir. France: Arte France, France 5, Image et Compagnie.

## MUSEUMS AND COMMEMORATIVE BUILDINGS

- The Verdun memorial located on the site of the Fleury-devant-Douaumont station.
- The German front-rear located in the township of Spincourt.
- Fort Douaumont.
- The ossuary of Douaumont.
- Fort Vaux.
- The destroyed village of Fleury.

# IMPROVE YOUR GENERAL KNOWLEDGE

## IN A BLINK OF AN EYE !

## www.50minutes.com